Killing Bill O'Reilly

The LEFT tried to KILL BILL'S CAREER! They failed!
Bill IS back with a VENGEANCE!

The LEFT tried to KILL BILL'S CAREER!
Their mission was to bring down Bill O'Reilly.
They failed!
To the LEFT'S chagrin and consternation, Bill IS back with a
VENGEANCE!

My book honors Bill O'Reilly.

In my judgment,
Bill is the nation's
greatest journalist
and political commentator!

Richard W. Linford

Killing Bill O'Reilly

The LEFT tried TO KILL BILL'S CAREER! They failed!

Bill IS back with a VENGEANCE!

The author. I work at being a good husband, dad, grandpa, neighbor, church and community servant, attorney, artist, and writer.

Killing Bill O'Reilly

The LEFT tried TO KILL BILL'S CAREER!

They failed!

Bill IS back with a VENGEANCE!

1. The LEFT.

2. The LEFT went out of their way to marginalize Bill O'Reilly.

3. Thought they had killed his career.

4. The LEFT, the Democrats, Disaffected Republicans, the Establishment, the Swamp, the Obama holdovers, the Deep state, all whom Bill called out for their sins of commission and omission, to their chagrin and consternation, now find that Bill is back from the journalism land of the dead!

5. The LEFT, the Liberal Media, in particular CNN, MSNBC, The New York Times, The Washington Post, NBC, to their like chagrin and consternation, not to be redundant, now find that Bill is resurrected from the journalism land of the dead.

6. Not only is his career rejuvenated, Bill is more vocal than ever about the LEFT Liberal Media, CNN, MSNBC, NBC, The New York Times, and others, calling out the Democrats, and Disaffected Republicans and lukewarm Independents, calling out the Establishment, the Swamp, the Obama holdovers, the Deep state, railing about the failure of journalistic and political ethics and standards, about the lack of civility, about the year-long fake news destroy POTUS at all costs Russians did it narrative, about email-gate, and China-gate, and Russia-gate, and Uranium-gate, and Clinton's predations-gate, and "finally" the Clinton dynasty demise, about healing a racial and an ideologically divided country.

7. POTUS TRUMP.

8. POTUS Trump has thrown his support to Roy Moore because Roy said he didn't do it.

9. Bill O'Reilly likewise said he didn't do it.

10. POTUS Trump no doubt will say the same about Bill.

11. Bill O'Reilly IS back with a VENGEANCE.

12.William James O'Reilly Jr.

13.Born. September 10, 1949.

14.Born in New York City, New York, U.S.A.

15.Lived on Long Island.

16.Parents.
17.William James O'Reilly Sr.
18.Angela "Ann" O'Reilly.

19.Education.

20.Marist College, University of London, Boston University, Harvard University.

21.Attended Catholic school.

22.Attended Marist College in Poughkeepsie, New York.

23.Major: History.

24.University of London for his junior year.

25.1971 graduated with honors.

26.Miami – 2 years teaching high school.

27.Boston University.

28.Master's degree in broadcast journalism.

29.Harvard University.

30.Master's degree in public administration.

31.**Website.** https://www.billoreilly.com/ Sign up. Bill is back.

32.Occupation.

33.American journalist.

34.Media heavyweight.

35.Political commentator.

36.Political savant.

37.Giant at Fox News

38.Television host.

39.Reporter.

40.Author.

41.Politics.

42.Republican prior to 2001.

43.Independent 2001 until the present.

44.Registered with the Independent Party of New York.

45.Conservative.

46.Immediate Family.
47.Spouse. Maureen McPhilmy. (Married 1996. Divorced 2011.)
48.Children. 2

49.Work experience in television news.

50.TV news career included:

51.Scranton, Pennsylvania.

52.Dallas.

53.Denver.

54.Portland.

55.Boston.

56.1980 New York anchored his own program.

57.CBS news correspondent.

58.1986 ABC News.

59.Awarded two Emmy Awards.

60.Awarded two National Headliner Awards.

61.1989 joined nationally syndicated Inside Edition.

62.Hired by Fox News Channel.

63.Hosted own show "The O'Reilly Factor."

64."THE O'REILLY FACTOR FORMAT.

65.Interviews.

66.Commentary.

67.Hottest issues.

68.Controversy.

69.Described as the "No Spin Zone."

70.2001. Most watched cable news program.

71. 2002 to 2009 also pushed a weekly syndicated newspaper column and national radio show "The Radio Factor."

72. Fox News Channel.

73. He joined in 1996.

74. He hosted The O'Reilly Factor until 2017.

75. Accusations and Fox News Termination.
76. American civil law is designed such that those who are "harmed," who sue, or threaten suit, are paid money to compensate them either by way of settlement or adjudication.
77. Accusations against Bill for sexual harassment were made.
78. Bill and Fox News elected to settle and pay money.
79. The New York Times broke the news that he paid a number of women to settle sexual harassment lawsuits.
80. Six suits were settled for plus minus $50 million.
81. With the sixth, the sexual harassment hue and cry became inordinately loud.
82. Fox News lost half of its advertisers (one list contains 60 companies lost) in a week.
83. Bill took a vacation.
84. The Murdochs terminated Bill's employment.

85. Bill's Response to Accusations.

86. Bill denies the allegations.

87. Denies any misconduct.

88. Claims the Times story is "a malicious smear."

89. "I have been in the broadcast business for 43 years with 12 different companies, and not one time was there any complaint filed against me. Nothing. Zero. So I think my track record speaks for itself."

90. No disputes have gone to court.

91. Bill said "he settled to avoid prolonged publicity that would have harmed his children."

92. See Bill O'Reilly tells Glenn Beck he blames The NY Times, CNN, and Media Matters for a "hit job" against him, https://www.mediamatters.org/video/2017/10/23/bill-oreilly-tells-glenn-beck-he-blames-ny-times-cnn-and-media-matters-hit-job-against-him/218302

93. See Bill O'Reilly comes to Bill O'Reilly's defense,The Washington Post, Democracy Dies in Darkness, Paul Farhi, October 24, https://www.washingtonpost.com/lifestyle/style/bill-oreilly-swings-back-at-his-accusers-in-sexual-harassment-cases/2017/10/24/e8700246-b82b-11e7-a908-a3470754bbb9_story.html?utm_term=.c936514eea81

94. Regarding the allegations:

95. Bill knows whether he is guilty of not.

96. He says he didn't do what is alleged.

97. He and Fox News paid plus minus $50 million in cash and settled legal claims.

98. That's what we do in America when there is a civil matter.

99. And famous people pay more money than non-famous people

100.We don't fight a duel with pistols or swords.

101.We don't fight physically.

102.The plaintiffs lawyer up.

103.They send letters and accuse.

104.They usually draft a complaint.

105.They litigate.

106.Defendants pay cash to plaintiffs either as compelled by the court or by way of settlement.

107.If they win in court, they don't pay.

108.Plaintiffs often end up paying attorney fees if they lose.

109.Another ramification of sexual harassment allegations, the harasser suffers loss of respect in the community and often loses his or her job.

These kinds of matters are tried in the press

to the harm of the families of the innocent or the guilty.

110.More of Bill's perspective:

111.Bill "O'Reilly has repeatedly said the potential impact on his children is a major reason for his outrage over the [New York] Times report.

112."The pain it brings to my children is indescribable. I would give up my life to protect my children, but I find myself unable to protect them because of things that are being said about me, their father.

113."This is horrible what I went through, horrible what my family went through." Bill said the report was "politically and financially motivated" and that he could "prove it with shocking information but I'm not going to sit here in a courtroom for a year and a half and let my kids get beaten up every single day of their lives by a tabloid press."

114."O'Reilly, on his website, said the [New York] Times, doesn't care about children and is willing to run a story based on anonymous sources even though "families are devastated."
115. "So and so said, so and so told me," O'Reilly said of the use of unnamed sources.
116. "That's what they do to [POTUS] Trump every day and that's why [POTUS] Trump is furious. That's why the President of the United States calls out The New York Times by name. ... the culture war is that intense.
117. "Bottom line on this is that my enemies who want to silence me have made my life extremely difficult.
118. See Bill O'Reilly is 'mad at God' for sexual harassment scandal, William Cummings, USA TODAY, October 24, 2017, https://www.usatoday.com/story/money/business/2017/10/24/bill-oreilly-mad-god-sexual-harassment-report/795331001/

119. Bill says he is mad at God.

120. Bill said: "You know, am I mad at God? Yeah, I'm mad at him. I wish I had more protection. I wish this stuff didn't happen. I can't explain it to you. If I die tomorrow and I get an opportunity, I'll say why'd you guys work me over like that? Didn't know my children were going to be punished? And they're innocent." (Ibid.)

121. So what to do?

122. Pay money.

123. Again, that is what we do in America.

124. What's at stake?

125. For Bill O'Reilly, some pretty rough times dealing with accusations.

126. For the nation, we're all caught up in the contention.

127. One side is elated POTUS Trump won.

128. One side can't get over it.

129. So what is wisdom?

130. How do we bring our divided nation together?

131. What are the solutions, the principles, for our day?

132. Who has some helpful answers?

133. For the RIGHT, Bill O'Reilly is a person to listen to.

134. For the LEFT, Bill O'Reilly, like POTUS Trump, is a person to reckon with.

135. For sexual harassment, if six multi-million dollar lawsuit women are telling the truth or telling falsehoods, the response today in the media and in our culture is to believe all of them. At the same time, media hosts at LEFT and RIGHT leaning media companies, and especially "The View," continue to tear Into Bill.

136. Right or wrong, they say "Bill O'Reilly: 'God Is Mad at You" by Clare Palo, October 24, 2017. https://www.thedailybeast.com/the-view-co-hosts-slam-bill-oreilly-and-fox-news, and you have little if any right to be mad at God.

137. The O'Reilly Factor.

138. Bill's cable television news and talk show for years has been The O'Reilly Factor.

139. A 60 minutes HDTV show.

140. A production of Fox News.

141. First episode date October 7, 1996.

142. Began airing on Fox News in 2001.

143. Last aired April 21, 2017 at time of Bill's firing by the Murdochs and Fox News.

144. Bill was host.
145. He was host of one of the highest-rated cable shows in history -- the O'Reilly Factor which was usually pre-recorded unless breaking news warranted otherwise.
146. Presidential debates and presidential addresses aired live.
147. Bill's catch phrase used to begin his show?
148. Caution!
You are about to enter the No Spin Zone.
The Factor begins right now!"
149. Bill's professional guests included people like Eric Bolling, Monica Crowley, Bernie Goldberg, Greg Gutfeld, E.D. Hill, Laura Ingraham, John Kasich, Michelle Malkin, Dana Perino, Geraldo Rivera, Tony Snow, Juan Williams.

150. As an old broadcaster, my criticism of The O'Reilly Factor show is pointed?

151. Bill would have blessed our viewer lives markedly if he had early on gotten rid of his regular professional guests and substituted real people like Larry King did on Larry King Live.

152. After the first one or two shows the presence of the professional guests became same old same old and detracted from Bill's show.

153. My hope is that Bill will forever avoid professional guests like the plague I think they are.

154. They, to a man and woman, were and still are light weights compared to Bill and several of them have unjustly ridden Bill's coat tails.

155. Hopefully, Bill, like Rush Limbaugh, will be the sole focal point going forward.

156. Notwithstanding, periodic Larry King Live interviews with prominent people will always be of great interest.

157. I mentioned that Bill claims the LEFT carried out a hit job on him.

158. Among others, Bill defines the LEFT as The New York Times, CNN, Media Matters, The Washington Post, the Democrats, and Disaffected Republicans, the Obama holdovers, the Establishment, and the deep state, and he is right in saying that this "LEFT" has marginalized him for a short time.

159. Why their angry focus on taking Bill out of the media equation?

160. Past and present, Bill has called out the media and political LEFT.

161. Bill has held their egregious fake news and dishonest sins of omission and commission up to the light of day.

162. Perhaps more important, Bill was a primary reason Donald J. Trump was elected POTUS.

163. He gave POTUS Trump a media platform, interviewing him multiple times during the 2016 campaign.

164. His response was straight forward and even handed when he was asked why he gave POTUS Trump so much airtime.

165. He said, I asked Hillary and Bernie and they would not come on the show.

166. The New York Times did not go easy on Bill.

167. "O'Reilly was fired after a report in The New York Times revealed he, Fox News and parent company 21st Century Fox had paid millions of dollars over the years to settle sexual harassment and other inappropriate behavior made against him, all of which he denied."

168. "The news, which came as the network was still reeling from a sexual harassment scandal that forced out former Fox News Chairman Roger Ailes, resulted in advertisers fleeing O'Reilly's show."

169. "Fox News ultimately decided to fire O'Reilly, not even letting him say goodbye to his audience – the ultimate TV indignity – after he'd served for more than two decades as the face of the network's primetime lineup."

170. Today, much to the LEFT'S chagrin and consternation, Bill's powerful political commentary and journalism career is back from the dead!

171. Chagrin means annoyance, displeasure, distress, embarrassment, exasperation, humiliation, irritation, vexation at having failed to take Bill out permanently.

172. Consternation means feelings of alarm, anxiety, astonishment, discomposure, dismay, disquiet, distress, fear, fright, panic, perturbation, distress, disquiet, discomposure, shock.

173. The left is disturbed to say the least at the prospect of Bill O'Reilly gaining ground against them.

174. I'm sure it looked for a time to the LEFT like Bill O'Reilly's career was dead and gone, that Bill O'Reilly had ridden off into the sunset for good.

175. NOT SO!

176. Bill is not going away.

177. Witness his No Spin News podcast.

178. Witness his interview with Sean Hannity.

179. Bill is no doubt building a massive data base of followers.

180. Whether he returns to Fox News or another network remains to be seen.

**181. He never left the game as an Author. Some of his books
are:**
182. Bill O'Reilly Culture Warrior.
183. Bill O'Reilly.
184. Give Please a Chance.
185. Hitler's Last Days.
186. Keep it Pithy.
187. Kennedy's Last Days.
188. Killing England: The Brutal Struggle
for American Independence.
189. Killing Jesus.
190. Killing Kennedy.
191. Killing Lincoln.
192. Killing Patton.
193. Killing Reagan.
194. Killing the Rising Sun.

195. Others?

196. Legends Lies The Real West.

197. Lincoln's Last Days.

198. Old School: Life in the Sane Lane.

199. Pinheads and Patriots.

200. The Day the President was Shot.

201. The Day the World Went Nuclear.

202. The O'Reilly factor.

203. The No Spin Zone.

204. Those Who Trespass.

205. The Murdochs

206. They knew about any accusations.

207. They helped pay the accusers.

208. They terminated Bill.

209. Maybe he will join Fox News again.

210. If he does, it will no doubt be for an immense amount of money.

**211. On the flip side, maybe Bill has a huge lawsuit against Fox
and the Murdochs for wrongful termination.
(A case hard and expensive to litigate, though, given the
plethora of accusations and huge earlier payouts.)**
212. Then again --

Depends on what kind of payout he got when he left
and what kind of conditions he had to sign
in order to effect a huge settlement
and what kind of new deal he might negotiate.

Depends on the facts.

213. And Then There Was Roger Eugene Ailes

214. Roger was an American television executive.

215. He was a media consultant for POTUS Nixon, Reagan, H.W. Bush, Trump, and for Rudy Giuliani's mayoral campaign.

216. He was Chairman of Fox Television Stations, CEO of Fox News, Chair of 20th Television, MyNetwork TV, and Fox Business Network.

217. He was brought low by sexual harassment allegations.

218. He was brought low by conflict with the Murdochs.

219. Andrea Tantaros filed a lawsuit in 2016 for sexual harassment, accusing Ailes, O'Reilly, and Scott Brown.

220. Some Huge Dollars Changed Hands.

At the heart of each matter was the objective to knock Bill O'Reilly off "The Factor."

221. Roger Ailes got a $40 million severance when he left Fox.

222. O'Reilly got a $25 million severance when he left Fox.

223. Gretchen Carlson who filed against Ailes got $20 million.

224. Again, "The mission was to bring down Bill O'Reilly."

225. It almost succeeded.

226. 'The mission was to bring down Bill O'Reilly': The final days of a Fox News superstar, https://www.washingtonpost.com/lifestyle/style/the-mission-was-to-bring-down-bill-oreilly-the-final-days-of-a-fox-news-superstar/2017/04/21/00862918-2601-11e7-bb9d-8cd6118e1409_story.html?utm_term=.1923d1574688

227. Media Matters and Being a Good Mentor to Women
228. Bill says "There was a sponsor boycott engineered by Media Matters, the radical left group, and the sponsor boycott unsettled some people at Fox News," said Bill.
229. O'Reilly states that he did "absolutely nothing wrong."
230. See Bill O'Reilly Says He Was
A Good Mentor To Women Working At Fox News, Rebecca Shapiro, https://www.huffingtonpost.com/entry/bill-oreilly-fox-news-mentor-women_us_59c348cbe4b063b25317d4d6

231. Is Fox News Rehabbing Bill O'Reilly?

232. Looks like it given the Sean Hannity Interview?

233. Focus of the interview? The "far-left conspiracy" that brought Bill down

and tried to bring Sean down?

234. The result of the O'Reilly Hannity

interview for Fox and Sean?

"A star-studded jolt in viewership."

235. "Sean Hannity. Bill O'Reilly. The powerful opinions you have to hear on the hot topics that have America talking."

236. "The interview you don't want to miss is only on Hannity."

237. Several say Fox and owners and Sean sold their souls when they gave Bill a platform?

238. Several say they arranged the interview for one reason?

239. To take down Rachel Maddow?

240. See Why is Fox News rehabbing Bill O'Reilly with a Hannity interview, https://www.thedailybeast.com/why-is-fox-news-rehabbing-bill-oreilly-with-a-hannity-interview

241. What are Bill's choices?

242. Keep operating his podcast?

243. Keep on keeping on calling out the LEFT, the Democrats, and disaffected Republicans?

244. Keep on supporting POTUS Trump as long as he keeps his election promises?

245. Accept a position with another media company network?

246. Start his own Media outlet competing with The New York Times, The Washington Post, CNN, MSNBC?

247. Work with Sean Hannity and start a new Media outlet?

248. Work with Glenn Beck of the Blaze and start a new Media outlet?

249. Join with the Murdochs again at Fox News?

250. On the flip side, maybe a huge lawsuit against them for wrongful termination?

251. On the flip side, maybe a huge lawsuit against his accusers?

252. Keep on keeping on selling books via his podcast and otherwise?

253. Cut a deal with Simon and Schuster or a like book seller?

254. All of the above?

255. Some of the above?

256. None of the above?

257. See Sean Hannity asks Bill to 'come back' to Fox News. http://www.nydailynews.com/entertainment/tv/sean-hannity-asks-bill-o-reilly-back-fox-news-article-1.3505146

258. Conservative Media Network Newsmax and CEO Chris Ruddy talking to Bill.

259. See Conservative media network Newsmax is in talks with Bill O'Reilly for cable show, November 1, 2017, THE WEEK, http://theweek.com/speedreads/734742/conservative-media-network-newsmax-talks-bill-oreilly-cable-show

260. **According to CEO Chris Ruddy,** "O'Reilly's show would air on Newsmax TV, the conservative media company's three-year old network, which currently reaches 35 million households. The network is also in talks with other cable carriers to expand its viewership. … Newsmax

remains optimistic about O'Reilly's appeal …: We don't think Bill O'Reilly's career is over. He does have a market. We're very interested and exploring looking at that. He's a significant talent. … In March, The Atlantic published a profile of [CEO Chris] Ruddy that referred to him as "an unofficial conduit from the inner sanctum of the presidency to the outside world." Ruddy is considered a close friend of President Trump's and has been seen in the past dining with Trump as well as former White House chief strategist Stephen Bannon." (Ibid.)

261. Demeanor and Commentary.

262. Bill is outspoken.

263. At times he is Incendiary.

264. Bill is said by some of his detractors to be disrespectful, homophobic, insensitive, racist, and sexist.

265. Response to such accusations?

266. All media heavyweights face immense pressure and criticism.

267. Anything is thought by the unscrupulous as fair game to destroy or steal their ratings and commensurate ad revenue.

268. Bill O'Reilly Outspoken Quotes.

269. ACLU IS DANGEROUS. Called out the ACLU as "the most dangerous organization in the United States of America right now," referring to the ACLU as a "terrorist group" and "fascist organization."

270. AFGHANISTAN. "The ravages of a seemingly endless war have kept the United States mired in South Asia for over 16 years. In August, U.S. President Donald Trump proposed a new solution to the intractable conflict in Afghanistan. The new strategy would focus not on meeting a specific deadline but rather on achieving the conditions necessary to bring peace to the war-torn country. To that end, [POTUS] Trump urged India to play a greater role in Afghanistan's economic development. He also had a few choice words for Pakistan." November 21, 2017.

271. AMERICA IS IN THE LULL BEFORE THE STORM. "It's clear to me we're in a lull before the storm that coming up will be some kind of horrific confrontation with forces that hate the USA and want to hurt us badly. I also believe we're not prepared to face that test."

272. AMERICA IS NOT PREPARED TO FACE AN ENEMY THAT WANTS TO EXTIRMINATE US. We're simply not prepared to face an enemy who wants to exterminate us. And that makes us have a huge weakness. And the enemy knows it."

273. AMERICA TODAY IS CONFUSED AND IN A TERROR, CULTURE, AND MEDIA WAR. AMERICAN MEDIA IS WITHOUT PROFESSIONAL STANDARDS. "America today is a confused society caught up in a terror war, a culture war, and a media war where honesty and professional standards have vanished."

274. AMERICANS ADMIRE ACHIEVEMENT. "The Republican leadership, including President Trump, should understand that voters are now cynical – disgusted with both parties. Only positive legislation will turn that around. Thus tax reform becomes vital to the GOP. The party must get it passed or Democrats will win next year's mid/term elections by a wide margin. Americans admire achievement. The GOP has little this year. [The Dems have none – nothing – nothing – zip – to show for their time in office since POTUS Trump was inaugurated. Hence the call to pass meaningful legislation to make us FREE, SAFE, and PROSPEROUS!] November 8, 2017.

275. ANTHEM PROTEST PROPAGANDA BY CNN.

276. "CNN is now branding the anthem/kneeling by some pro football players as a "civil rights" protest. Very interesting. The reason the situation is being portrayed that way by CNN is that if you now criticize the players, you are actually demeaning "civil rights" therefore you are a racist. This is called "propaganda."

November 22, 2017.

277. ASIA FIVE NATION TRIP BY POTUS TRUMP. "This was all about economics and trade deals ... and it was about isolating North Korea. Trump's style, and I know this because I've known the guy for 30 years, is to try and become friends with folks. He feels that if he has that camaraderie and rapport he can make good deals, and that's what he did. Did he get any good deals? I don't know, but he says it was a successful trip." November 15, 2017.

278. BILL'S 9/11 RESPONSE IS NOT TO BE DENIGRATED. To Jeremy Glick, who accused Bill of using 9/11 for his own gain, Bill said "I've done more for the 9/11 families by their own admission. I've done more for them than you will ever hope to do, so keep your mouth shut." Bill said to "Cut his [Jeremy Glick's] mic."

279. BIRTH CONTROL IS EQUATED WITH SEX. To Sandra Fluke, he said "You want me to give you my hard-earned money so you can have sex?" Equating birth control with sex.

280. BLACK LIVES MATTER IS KILLING AMERICANS.
Bill said "Black Lives Matter is killing Americans."

281. BREXIT. "The EU Withdrawal Bill that will transfer EU rules and norms into British law, a crucial part of the Brexit process, has entered the lower House of Commons for debate and is scheduled for final approval in early 2018." November 16, 2017.

282. CHICAGO SOUTH SIDE IS A DISASTER. He said "If you've ever been to the South Side of Chicago, I mean, it's a disaster, all right? It's like Haiti, …

283. CLINTONS. "Hillary Clinton [AND BILL] continues to face a slew of scandals - …" November 7, 2017.

284. CLINTONS – NEW INVESTIGATION. November 14, 2017.

285. CORRUPT MEDIA.

"I have never seen any institution in America that is so corrupt, so bitterly ideological, that's so one-sided," Hannity opined. "All they want to do is destroy this president." O'Reilly responded, "We're living in a time with no more journalistic rules, and I can back that up 50 different ways, but I'm not going to bore everybody tonight. But I will someday."

286. COURT ANARCHY? [Maybe so! Anarchy is the condition of a society, entity, group of people, or a single person that rejects hierarchy.] "Bill began Tuesday's No Spin News with a couple of breaking news items from the West Coast. ..., Liberal Federal Judge William Orrick has blocked the Trump administration's plan to withhold federal funds from sanctuary cities that don't cooperate with immigration authorities. "Judge Orrick says the administration can't do that," Bill reported, "because only Congress has the right to regulate who gets money. It's not a terrible legal argument, but if you violate the law the Justice Department can certainly punish you. This will be litigated and I hope the Justice Department will file a court action against San Francisco and other places because they are violating federal law." November 21, 2017.

287. CULTURAL COLLAPSE? "To debate the question of whether we are witnessing a collapsing culture, Bill welcomed Julie Alvin, who oversees lifestyle coverage for all of Time Inc. She pointedly blamed President Trump for the decline in civility. "There has been an erosion of decency and respect," Alvin said, "and the most glaring example of that is the person sitting in the White House. He starts fights with foreign leaders and football players and congressmen. The fact that he was voted into office is an indication of our culture collapse." November 21, 2017.

288. DESTRUCTION OF DUE PROCESS AND INTELLECTUALLY DISHONEST NANCY PELOSI. "Nancy Pelosi is now promoting 'due process' because John Conyers and Al Franken are in trouble. She's correct about innocent until proven guilty but amazingly hypocritical. If Pelosi doesn't like you politics, she could not care less about due process. In 43 years of journalism, I rank Nancy Pelosi in the top five of intellectually dishonest politicians that I've witnessed." November 27, 2017.

289. DESTRUCTION OF DUE PROCESS BY THE MEDIA. "The media, both social and commercial, has destroyed due process in America. Charlatans and deceivers well understand that all negative headlines are now convictions – a person under siege is defenseless in the court of public opinion. This is great news for sleazy lawyers who capitalize on fear of the media." November 27, 2017.

290. ETHICS INVESTIGATION OF AL FRANKEN. "Senate Majority leader Mitch McConnell is calling for an ethics investigation of Al Franken, a senator from Minnesota. That after a Los Angeles newscaster accused Franklin of untoward behavior on a 2006 USO tour. Back in my first few years at FNC, Franken, not yet a politician, routinely lied about me trying to damage Fox News." November 16, 2017.

291. FREEDOM OF SPEECH THREATENED BY EXTORTION PRATICED BY "MEDIA MATTERS." "Sean Hannity again being attacked by Media Matters, the far left propaganda group that starts sponsor boycotts. Some of Hannity's supporters are themselves boycotting businesses that give in to the extortion practiced by Media Matters. It doesn't matter what the issue is, threats have no place in our society. Yet they are embraced by bad people like the zealots who follow and staff Media Matters." November 13, 2017.

292. GAY MARRIAGE LEADS TO POLY-AMORPHOUS AND POLYGAMOUS MARRIAGES. He claimed "legalizing gay marriage would lead to 'poly-amorphous' marriage, including not only polygamous marriage, but also interspecies marriage."

293. HAITI JUST NEVER GETS BETTER. He said "I've been to Haiti a couple of times. I support some charities there, but Haiti just never gets better, no matter how much money you put in there because they don't have a system."

294. HANNITY FEELS HE AND O'REILLY ARE VICTIMS OF LEFT EFFORTS TO SILENCE THEM. "Hannity appears to feel that he and O'Reilly have both become victims of liberals looking to silence them, and have found some kinship with him over that.

295. HAPPINESS AND PEACE. "On Friday, everyone can watch a special edition of the No Spin News, so I hope you'll take the time. Finally, we wish you a great Thanksgiving; I hope the day brings you happiness and peace. By Bill O'Reilly." November 22, 2017.

296. HONOR THE FLAG. "From what I can ascertain, the NFL players who are kneeling believe the USA generally oppresses minorities especially in the justice system. That is not an uncommon belief in left wing precincts. But the issue turns on honoring the American flag, not social justice. You can absolutely respect the flag and want improvements made to all of our systems. But to dishonor the flag publicly offends the majority of Americans and they have a perfect right to protest the football players without being branded anti-civil rights. Somebody tell CNN. November 22, 2017.

297. HAPPY THANKSGIVING. "Happy Thanksgiving 2017!" November 24, 2017.

298. I AM ALIVE AND THE SPIN STOPS HERE. "I'm here, I'm alive, and the spin stops here."

299. I NEVER MISTREATED ANYONE UNDER MY WATCH. "Nobody is a perfect person, but I can go to sleep at night knowing very well that I never mistreated anyone under my watch over 42 years."

300. ILLEGAL IMMIGRATION. "The progressive left, some call it the far left, does not want to restrain illegal immigration … they want the E.U. system." August 7, 2017.

301. ILLEGAL IMMIGRATION. "There is a flurry of illegal immigration stories in play and there is a common denominator to all of them: defying the law." (August 7, 2017.)

302. I'LL COME BACK. Sean Hannity said "Come back. Will you come back? Hannity asked. "I'll come back," O'Reilly answered, after joking that the two were due for a fishing trip first.

303. IF INNOCENT WHY DIDN'T BILL SUE HIS ACCUSERS? BECAUSE AS A PUBLIC FIGURE YOU CAN'T WIN! "Because you can't win those lawsuits. If you're a public figure, you cannot win them."

304. INTERNET IS BEING USED BY THE FAR LEFT TO SPEW PROPAGANDA. "Also, the far left is making great use of the Internet, libeling their opponents and spewing out anti-American propaganda all day long."

305. JENNIFER MOORE, RAPE MURDER VICTIM, WAS MORONIC. He referred to Jennifer Moore, a rape murder victim, who prior to her death was wearing a miniskirt and halter top with bare midriff, as "moronic" "for getting her car towed in New York City while she was drunk."

306. KAEPERNICK PROTEST IS MOB MENTALITY AND ACTION.
"It's a mob mentality. It is an anti-Trump demonstration. That's what it's morphed into. .. The [National Football] League and the owners have lost control of [the protest]."

307. KATE STEINLE. "Finally, the pope. I would very much like to speak with him. And if I can arrange that, I would like to bring the family of Kate Steinle with me. ... I think I could persuade the pope that providing protection and enforcing settled law is certainly not un-Christian. What is against the tenets of Jesus is to allow chaos that harms innocent people, like Kate Steinle and her family." Bill O'Reilly's Lecture To Pope Francis Was Our Most Outrageous Quote Last Week, Post, March 6, 2016,
http://www.newshounds.us/bill_o_reilly_s_lecture_to_pope_francis_was_our_most_outrageous_quote_last_week_030616

308. KATE'S LAW. "Kate's Law, ... is finally on track after years. I am not on television anymore to lend that club but I wanted you guys to know this is coming to fruition, and I do believe it will be law. The fact is that 167 congress people do not want to protect you. This was an easy vote." July 3, 2017.

309. LEFT USES RACISM AS A WEDGE. "The media and the entertainers drive it. A year ago, you did not hear the words 'white supremacist.' It was white privilege.

310. LEFT WANTS TO TAKE POWER FROM THE WHITE ESTABLISHMENT. He said "the left wants power taken away from the white establishment."

311. LEFT-WING JOURNALS ARE FILLED WITH PROPAGANDA. O'Reilly dismissed major urban newspapers as "left-wing journals" that coordinate coverage. … A lot of people believe propaganda and there's nothing we can do about it."

312. LIES ARE FED TO US DAILY BY THE MEDIA INCLUDING BY NBC NEWS AND THE NY TIMES. "We are being lied to on a daily basis by the media as far left fanatics have assumed power in places like NBC News and The New [York] Times."

313. MARK CUBAN IS MORE THAN MISGUIDED IN DISTRIBUTING THE FAIRY TALE MOVIE 'LOOSE CHANGE.'
"Here's how bad things are: There's a movie called "Loose Change" that asserts hundred, if not thousands, of Americans colluded to kill their fellow citizens on 9/11. That Al Qaeda didn't attack us, we essentially attacked ourselves. This fairy tale ranks up there with the Holocaust deniers on the vicious scale. Yet Mark Cuban is going to distribute the film so people all over the world can see it.

314. MEDIA IS CORRUPT. "Most Americans know the media is corrupt according to a new poll from Quinnipiac University. And those folks who do not believe that are deceiving themselves. Here's a perfect example: media coverage of Roy Moore is wall to wall. But the corruption trial of Senator Robert Menendez, a democrat, has received scant attention even though there are lurid accusations as there are with Moore." November 5, 2017.

315. MITT ROMNEY WAS AN "IN THE MINORITY ESTABLISHMENT CANDIDATE." He said Mitt Romney was an establishment candidate. The "white establishment is now in the minority."

316. MOVIE "LOOSE CHANGE" IS GARBAGE AND YOU THROW GARBAGE AWAY. "Now as I told Mr. [Mark] Cuban, I'm not buying that. You don't refute garbage. You throw garbage away. This stupid thing will be used by America haters all over the world and will damage this country. Also, any slick technician can make a propaganda film. Just ask the Nazis."

317.NEWS AND SPORTS CONSUMPTION BY AMERICANS.
"There is a significant change occurring in the way Americans consume news and sports. The powerful National Football League is losing viewers and fans. Last night's Monday Night football game was low-rated and team owners are furious that revenue is falling largely due to social justice on-field protests by some players. On the news front, the three nightly network broadcasts yield very little influence anymore. … Cable news is largely partisan. … The result is that millions of folks are simply tuning out, going into cyberspace to secure information. That benefits this website but divides Americans because truth is not the goal of many online operations. Opinions are replacing hard facts in the national discourse." November 14, 2017.

318.NORTH KOREA URGED BY POTUS TRUMP TO 'MAKE A DEAL' REGARDING NUCLEAR WEAPONS PROGRAM. "President Trump said Tuesday in South Korea that "good progress" is happening on North Korea and he urged the regime to "come to the table" and "make a deal." November 8, 2017.

319.OPIOID CRISIS. "The economic cost of the opioid epidemic was about $504 billion in 2015, which is more than six times higher than other studies from previous years. (This figure accounts for roughly 2.8 percent of gross domestic product.) November 20, 2017.

320.PEACE. Trump is a peacemaker in Asia. November 13, 2017.

321.PRAYER AFTER THE MASSACRE IN TEXAS. "So now the far left is mocking those who call for prayers after the massacre in a south Texas church. The foolish line of thinking is the victims were praying as they were murdered so what good does praying actually do? The loons want no theological solace or respect – they want action: strict federal gun control laws." November 7, 2017.

322.SANCTUARY CITIES. "California is suing the Trump administration for threatening to withhold funds for sanctuary cities, accusing the Justice Department of "pure intimidation" and arguing the state – not the federal government – should be the one to allocate its law enforcement resources." August 15, 2017.

323.STAR SPANGLED BANNER NOT RACIST. "There is a big lie being promoted by the California chapter of the NAACP and that is the false assertion that the Star Spangled Banner, our National Anthem, is a racist song. That is simply outrageous. The Star Spangled Banner was written 1814 by a 35 year old poet named Francis Scott Key. He was watching the Battle of Baltimore during the War of 1812 and was inspired to glorify the American flag which withstood a British bombardment." November 9, 2017.

324.TAX REFORM. "On Monday, President Trump called for major changes to the tax plans currently working their way through Congress. In a tweet sent from Asia, [POTUS] Trump said he is "proud" of lawmakers for getting "close" to approving a tax bill but added that he wants to see more tweaks." November 13, 2017.

325.THANKSGIVING CIVILITY IS IN JEOPARDY. "As we Americans approach Thanksgiving, a holiday that is unique to us, we find ourselves in the middle of a social civil war where civility and fairness has pretty much collapsed on the internet and in the media. No one is safe from verbal attacks, allegations have become convictions, and hatred consumes many of us. A good portion of America is actually worried about civility at the Thanksgiving dinner table this year. My analysis usually includes solutions but I have none on this day.

I try to keep my kids away from the hate but that's almost impossible. It's ironic that we are living in an age of political correctness where anything deemed offensive becomes a major event, yet the worst possible invective is actually being celebrated on social media. These are not good days for the country and things may get even worse. We are a nation divided ideologically and many citizens have become bitter. Who can we count on to reverse this awful circumstance? Who?

326.TOTALITARIAN LEFTWING NEWS NETWORKS AND JOURNALISTS WANT TO WIPE OUT FREE SPEECH. "These totalitarians [leftwing non –FNC cable news networks and leftwing journalists who coordinate among themselves] want to wipe out any speech with which they disagree."

327.TOXIC POLITICAL CLIMATE. "Tonight on the No Spin News we will discuss this further. We'll also talk with Greta van Susteren about the toxic political climate. We hope you are a Premium Member so you can get our video news analysis every day." November 22, 2017.

328.TRAYVON MARTIN DIED IN PART BECAUSE HE LOOKED LIKE A "GANGSTA." "The reason Trayvon Martin died is because he looked a certain way.

It wasn't based on skin color, if Trayvon Martin had been wearing a jacket ... and a tie ... I don't think George Zimmerman would have had

any problem with him. And that way is how "gangstas" look and therefore he got attention."

329.TRIAL BY MEDIA IS THE NORM SUPPLANTING TRIAL BY THE JUSTICE SYSTEM. "It is simply impossible to know the truth about all the allegations flying around the country involving famous people. Every American should clamor for justice in all cases of alleged wrongdoing – that's a given. As history shows us, once justice is replaced by totalitarianism, oppression takes over. In America, we now have trial by media. And, of course, the media can easily be manipulated and in some cases, the press is flat out corrupt. So you will not get justice on the internet, on TV or the radio. The court system is the only place where a fair hearing is even possible. And you'd better have a lot of cash on hand if you wind up there. The speed of allegations has changed everything in this world. Instantly, people can be harmed in profound ways. There is no caution or restraint in the communications world; only exposure." November 10, 2017.

330.TRUMP TWEETING. "The father of one of the three UCLA basketball players arrested for shop lifting in China, LaVar Ball, insulted President Trump after he secured the release of the man's son and the others, all of whom faced five year prison terms in China. In both cases, [POTUS] Trump tweeted his displeasure with the situations. Predictably, the hate Trump media hammered him for doing so, one nitwit on CNN even tried to make the China thing racial. We've come to a point where the President no longer has a right to express himself in the eyes of the media. It's an absurd situation that we will analyze further on the No Spin News tonight." November 20, 2017.

331.WAR REPORTING ACCUSATIONS ARE BOGUS. WAR REPORTING TRANSCRIPT: Bill DEFENDS his war reporting with Howie Kurtz, BOR Staff, February 22, 2015. "They are trying to impugn my career. They are trying to smear me and impugn my career. Nobody's gunna do that. If anybody contradicts what I have said about my reportage, they need to come on my program and look me in the eye. Eric Engberg is a coward. OK? He's a coward. He can come on and say 'hey Bill, This didn't happen. I was there, I was this'. I want David and I want you, Howie, to call up Engberg and ask him if he was there. I'd like to know if he was there, and if he was there, why he has no video."

332.WASHINGTON DC POLITICAL FIGHTING IS FIERCE WITH DEMOCRATS BENT ON DESTROYING REPUBLICANS. "In Washington, the political fighting is fierce. The Democrats are hell bent on destroying the Bush administration and making sure a Democrat sits in the White House the next time around. And while the Dems are focused, the Republicans are confused. It's hard to defend the chaos in Iraq. And it's hard to counter daily charges of corruption. The GOP is on the defensive 24/7."

333. WE WILL FIGHT BACK. "Hannity and I have discussed it off camera. We will fight back. You fought back when they came after you last spring. I didn't, and I should have."

334. WE WILL PROVE WHAT WE SAY. THERE IS MORE TO COME. "We're going to be able to prove what we say. There are more things to come."

335. WHITEHOUSE SHAKEUPS, SANCTUARY CITY CHAOS, DRUGS IN AMERICA. "You can't have chaos every day. And that's what we're experiencing here. It's not good for the country." August 1, 2017.

336. NEW PODCAST. "The banner which is displayed across the top of his site reads "Monday. No Spin News Returns, Bill O'Reilly Is Already Back With A New Podcast.

337. ONE OF BILL'S POINTED SPEECHES.

338. Bill O'Reilly rips 'open society' in speech at Economic Club

339. By K. AARON VAN OOSTERHOUT / H-P Correspondent

340. May 24, 2004

341. AMERICA IS BECOMING AN OPEN SOCIETY. BENTON TOWNSHIP -- America stands at the brink of becoming an "open society" where no rules apply, one of cable television's most popular news personalities warned Sunday.

342. AMERICA IS AT A SECULAR-TRADITIONAL CULTURAL DICHOTOMY – BROUGHT ON BY GAY MARRIAGE, LEGALIZED MEDICAL MARIJUANA, AND AN OPEN SOCIETY. Bill O'Reilly, host of Fox News' "The O'Reilly Factor," told the Economic Club of Southwestern Michigan that America is at a secular-traditional cultural dichotomy. It was brought on by gay marriage, legalized medical marijuana and what billionaire liberal George Soros terms "an open society."

343. ANECDOTE. To explain his own stance, O'Reilly told the crowd at Lake Michigan College's Mendel Center an anecdote from his past.

344. As a teenager, he had been a fan of the popular rock band The Doors. Attending one of their concerts, he said he saw standing in front of him a family of four: a mother, father, and

two young boys about 10 to 12 years old. Standing in front of them was a man smoking marijuana, and the smoke was drifting into the faces of the family.

345. The mother tapped the man on the shoulder and asked him to put out the joint, but the man refused, uttering an obscenity.

346. YOU'RE GOING TO PUT IT OUT OR SWALLOW IT! O'Reilly - there with a friend, "the Bear, who looked like a biker" - then tapped the man on the shoulder and told him, "you're gonna put it out, or you're gonna swallow it."

347. HE DID NOTHING WITHOUT THREAT OF PHYSICAL FORCE BECAUSE HE LIVED IN AN OPEN SOCIETY. Amidst laughter and applause from the crowd, O'Reilly squinted his blue eyes and said, "That guy did nothing (without the threat of physical force), because he lived in an 'open society.'"

348. IN AN OPEN SOCIETY PEOPLE DO WHAT THEY WANT WITHOUT FEAR OF BEING JUDGED. In an open society, O'Reilly said, individuals are allowed to do whatever they feel like doing, without fear of being judged by others.

349. I DON'T WANT THESE PEOPLE, QUASI-SOCIALISM, BREAK DOWN IN SOCIETY'S STRUCTURE, AND HOOLIGANS. "I don't want these guys," he said. "I don't want quasi-socialism. I don't want to break down structure so these hooligans can do what they want to do when they want to do it."

350. ACLU AND PLANNED PARENTHOOD ARE HOOLIGANS. Among the other "hooligans" he named were the American Civil Liberties Union and Planned Parenthood.

351.CONTEMPORARY PUBLIC EDUCATION IS NOT TEACHING CIVICS, AMERICAN GOVERNMENT AND HISTORY, IT IS TEACHING GAY MARRIAGE. He also decried contemporary public education, saying that instead of teaching children civics, American government and U.S. history, "It's teaching them about gay marriage, and how great it is."

352.MARRIAGE IS DEFINED AS A MAN AND A WOMAN. O'Reilly said of homosexual couples: "We'll give you the full rights under the law as a married couple, but we're not gonna give you the label marriage, because that is defined as a man and a woman."

353.O'Reilly talked of other current issues, most notably the war in Iraq.

354.THERE ARE EXCESSES IN THE WAR IN IRAQ. He detailed what he said were the war's successes and said he believed the Bush administration had "very good intentions" going into Iraq.
355. He then launched into the current dilemma: Should we stay or should we go?

356. DO NOT BABY-SIT THE IRAQIS. "We cannot baby-sit (the Iraqis)," he said to the applauding crowd. "Give them a chance, give them stability, but we should get out of there as soon as we can get the heck out of there."

357. IRAQI PEOPLE DO NOT APPRECIATE WHAT WE HAVE DONE. He explained his position, saying, "The majority of the Iraqi people do not appreciate what we've done for them."

358. U.S. MILITARY SHOULD SHIP OUT OF IRAQ [AND THE MIDDLE EAST] IMMEDIATELY. For that reason, O'Reilly said the U.S. military should ship out and not let another soldier die for that ungrateful nation. For good measure, he added three other reasons: the lack of weapons of mass destruction, the current Iraqi insurrection and the recent human rights violations at Abu-Ghraib prison.

359. He concluded the speech with a warning to the audience about the upcoming presidential election.

360. TERROR THREAT IS NOT GOING TO GO AWAY. "This terror threat's not going to go away," he said. "Figure out who Osama (bin Laden) wants elected, and vote for the other guy. I figured it out, and it's Ralph (Nader)" that bin Laden wants elected.

361. NADER HAS NO ANSWERS FOR PUBLIC SECURITY. Nader doesn't have any answers for public security issues, he said.

362. See Bill O'Reilly Reps Open Society, Speech at Economic Club, http://www.heraldpalladium.com/localnews/bill-o-reilly-rips-open-society-in-speech-at-economic/article_2189e905-1959-58d0-8157-bd2350b30ba2.html

363. See The former Fox News Anchor will be back with a new podcast Monday night, Opheli Garcia Lawler, http://www.thefader.com/2017/04/23/bill-oreilly-is-back-with-new-podcast

364. See https://www.billoreilly.com/video/video-of-the-day?vid=-732656056077846502

365. ADDED SOURCES.

366. Bill O'Reilly And Sean Hannity Blast "Liberal Fascists" In Fox News Chanel Interview, Lisa de Moraes, September 27, 2017, http://deadline.com/2017/09/bill-oreilly-sean-hannity-liberal-fascists-fox-news-channel-1202177853/

367. Bill O'Reilly appears on Fox News for first time since his ouster, Oliver Darcy, September 26, 2017, http://money.cnn.com/2017/09/26/media/oreilly-hannity-fox-news-interview/index.html

368. Bill O'Reilly Biography, https://www.biography.com/people/bill-oreilly-9542547

369. Bill O'Reilly comes to Bill O'Reilly's defense, The Washington Post, Democracy Dies in Darkness, Paul Farhi, October 24, https://www.washingtonpost.com/lifestyle/style/bill-oreilly-swings-back-at-his-accusers-in-sexual-harassment-cases/2017/10/24/e8700246-b82b-11e7-a908-a3470754bbb9_story.html?utm_term=.c936514eea81

370. Bill O'Reilly (Political Commentator), https://en.wikipedia.org/wiki/Bill_O%27Reilly_(political_commentator)

371. Bill O'Reilly returns to Fox News to point fingers and air grievances, Libby Hill, September 27, 2017,

http://www.latimes.com/entertainment/la-et-entertainment-news-updates-bill-o-reilly-returns-to-fox-news-to-1506532345-htmlstory.html

372. Bill O'Reilly says his firing at Fox News was a 'hit job,' Terence Cullen, September 19, 2017, http://www.nydailynews.com/news/national/bill-o-reilly-firing-fox-news-hit-job-article-1.3505888

373. Bill O'Reilly tells Glenn Beck he blames NY Times, CNN, and Media Matters for a "hit job" against him, https://www.mediamatters.org/video/2017/10/23/bill-oreilly-tells-glenn-beck-he-blames-ny-times-cnn-and-media-matters-hit-job-against-him/218302

374. Bill O'Reilly's Most Shocking Quotes: The Hoodie, ACLU Terrorists and Victim –Blaming, http://variety.com/2017/tv/news/bill-oreilly-wildest-quotes-1202390457/

375. BILL'S MESSAGE OF THE DAY, Approaching Thanksgiving, Bill O'Reilly, November 21, 2017, https://www.billoreilly.com/b/Approaching-Thanksgiving/936718942561134918.html

376. Bill's Website, https://www.billoreilly.com/

377. Fox News, Hating America, http://www.foxnews.com/story/2007/03/26/hating-america.html

378. Fox News, Hating America, Published March 26, 2007,
http://www.foxnews.com/story/2007/03/26/hating-america.html

379. TRANSCRIPT: Bill [O'Reilly] DEFENDS his war reporting
with Howie Kurtz, BOR Staff, February 22, 2015,
https://www.billoreilly.com/b/TRANSCRIPT:-Bill-DEFENDS-his-war-reporting-with-Howie-Kurtz/-383362269824416867.html

380. Bill O'Reilly is 'mad at God' for sexual harassment scandal,
William Cummings, USA TODAY, October 24, 2017,
https://www.usatoday.com/story/money/business/2017/10/24/bill-oreilly-mad-god-sexual-harassment-report/795331001/

381. eBooks and Books Catalog

382. Richard W. Linford

383. 2017

384. Following is a list of my book subjects and titles most of which are found at
385. <u>**www. amazon.com. Type Richard W. Linford or Richard Linford.**</u>

386. <u>ABS OF STEEL.</u> **HOW TO BUILD SIX-PACK ABS OF STEEL THE QUALITY REP WAY! Man or Woman! In the Privacy of your own home!**
387. https://www.amazon.com/HOW-BUILD-SIX-PACK-STEEL-QUALITY-ebook/dp/B010EM6MY6/ref=sr_1_85?ie=UTF8&qid=1502472532&sr=8-85&keywords=Richard+W.+Linford

388. <u>ADVERTISING. MARKETING.</u> **Jackalope Mindset: Focus on your Jackalope! Break through the social and media clutter. Sell yourself, your products and your services.**
389. https://www.amazon.com/Jackalope-Mindset-clutter-yourself-services-ebook/dp/B01LG786EW/ref=sr_1_35?ie=UTF8&qid=1502472693&sr=8-35&keywords=Richard+W.+Linford

390. <u>ANXIETY.</u> **<u>Marty and The UK Brexit High Anxiety Hotel and Restaurant. A short story. An allegory.</u>**

391. <u>BAKING SODA USES?</u> **325 ARM & HAMMER BAKING SODA USES??? (Socium Bicarbonate; Bi-carbonate Soda) USES THAT PEOPLE CLAIM WORK???**
392. https://www.amazon.com/325-HAMMER-BAKING-SODA-USES-ebook/dp/B011CF6U0K/ref=sr_1_6?ie=UTF8&qid=1502486878&sr=8-6&keywords=Richard+W+Linford

393. <u>BEST PRACTICE AND BEST PRACTICES.</u> **THE POWER OF BEST PRACTICE AND BEST PRACTICES.**
394. https://www.amazon.com/Power-Best-Practice-Practices/dp/1521361398/ref=sr_1_24?ie=UTF8&qid=1502473575&sr=8-24&keywords=Richard+W+Linford

395. <u>BLINDING FLASH OF THE OBVIOUS.</u> **IN SEARCH OF 500 NOT SO BLINDING AND BLINDING FLASHES OF THE OBVIOUS**
396. https://www.amazon.com/SEARCH-500-BLINDING-FLASHES-OBVIOUS-ebook/dp/B01N0EHXVM/ref=sr_1_9?ie=UTF8&qid=1505837336&sr=8-9&keywords=Richard+W.+Linford

397. <u>BRAIN POWER.</u> **Better Brain! Super Brain! Supercharge Your Brain! Supercharge Your Brain 1209 Ways!**

398. <u>BRAIN POWER.</u> **IQ+: How to increase your IQ and your personal power to get things done right now**

399. <u>BUSINESS TURNAROUND.</u> **HOW TO BEGIN TURNING YOUR BUSINESS AROUND IN 30 MINUTES: Save a fortune on consulting services!**
400. https://www.amazon.com/BEGIN-TURNING-BUSINESS-AROUND-MINUTES-ebook/dp/B011T55SUG/ref=sr_1_8?ie=UTF8&qid=1505837336&sr=8-8&keywords=Richard+W.+Linford

401. <u>BUSINESS TURNAROUND.</u> **Stop Strolling Around Naked In Your Business Empire Like "ALITTLEKINGLY". Begin to turn your business around now.**
402. https://www.amazon.com/Strolling-Around-Business-Empire-ALittle/dp/1575740206/ref=sr_1_36?ie=UTF8&qid=1505839392&sr=8-36&keywords=Richard+W.+Linford

403. <u>COMING OF AGE.</u> **I Am the Count of Monte Cristo: How to Field-dress your Deer – A short story.**

404. <u>CONCORD, CALIFORNIA.</u> **concord in the Son: honoring concord california.**

405. <u>DEATH AND SACRIFICE.</u> **Andrew Chipman's Christmas Angel, a novelette.**

406. <u>DISINTERMEDIATION.</u>
<u>INTERMEDIATION.</u> **Disintermediation, Intermediation, or Both: 200 steps to greater prosperity by eliminating or adding intermediaries.**
407. https://www.amazon.com/Disintermediation-Intermediation-Both-eliminating-intermediaries-ebook/dp/B01DMIJ0DY/ref=sr_1_27?ie=UTF8&qid=1505838733&sr=8-27&keywords=Richard+W.+Linford

408. <u>EMERGENCY PREPAREDNESS.</u> **Sleep While The Wind Blows! Survival Checklists! Prepare Now! When a disaster or emergency happens, your time for preparation is over!**

409. <u>FICTION.</u> **Andrew Chipman's Christmas Angel.**
410. https://www.amazon.com/Andrew-Chipmans-Christmas-Richard-LInford/dp/1575740176/ref=sr_1_38?ie=UTF8&qid=1505839508&sr=8-38&keywords=Richard+W.+Linford

411. <u>FICTION</u>. **JOSHUA REDSHIELD'S DNA AND THE ILLUMINATI? A TECHNOTHRILLER (JOSHUA REDSHIELD AND THE ILLUMINATI Book 1)**

412. <u>FICTION</u>. **The Young Marine and the Snow an allegory.**
413. https://www.amazon.com/Young-Marine-Snow-Allegory/dp/1575740192/ref=sr_1_37?ie=UTF8&qid=1505839508&sr=8-37&keywords=Richard+W.+Linford

414. <u>FICTION</u>. **Waiting with Brutus Caesar Anthony the 7th, William and Mary, for SAM THE MECHANIC MAN.**
415. https://www.amazon.com/Waiting-Brutus-Anthony-William-MECHANIC/dp/1521158010/ref=sr_1_32?ie=UTF8&qid=1505839176&sr=8-32&keywords=Richard+W.+Linford

416. <u>HABITS OF LOSERS</u>. **How to Lose! 70 habits of losers who abuse or lose friends, health, influence and money!**

417. <u>HEALTH</u>. **HIGH FRUCTOSE CORN SYRUP AND SUGAR BELLY.**
418. https://www.amazon.com/HIGH-FRUCTOSE-SYRUP-SUGAR-BELLY-ebook/dp/B01B554JAK/ref=sr_1_28?ie=UTF8&qid=1505838733&sr=8-28&keywords=Richard+W.+Linford

419. <u>JESUS CHRIST PAPERS. ANGELS</u>. **ARE SHOULDER ANGELS AMONG US? Yes. There are good and bad angels.**
420. https://www.amazon.com/ARE-SHOULDER-ANGELS-AMONG-US-ebook/dp/B00Q3GX8Q8/ref=sr_1_12?ie=UTF8&qid=1502487183&sr=8-12&keywords=Richard+W+Linford

421. <u>JESUS CHRIST PAPERS. ARTICLES OF FAITH</u>. **My 32 Articles of Faith in God the Father and His Son Jesus Christ: Based on Joseph Smith's 13 Articles of Faith, LDS Gospel Principles, and my understanding of the doctrine and Church of Jesus Christ.**

422. https://www.amazon.com/Articles-Faith-Father-Jesus-Christ-ebook/dp/B011DTKQSC/ref=sr_1_10?ie=UTF8&qid=150248718 3&sr=8-10&keywords=Richard+W+Linford

423. JESUS CHRIST PAPERS. **BEHOLD THE MAN: Jesus is The Christ, The Great Jehovah, The Holy Messiah who soon will come!**

424. JESUS CHRIST PAPERS. **Meditations on Jesus The Christ and the Book of Mormon, Book of Moroni**
425. https://www.amazon.com/Meditations-Jesus-Christ-Mormon-Moroni-ebook/dp/B01MDJT7R7/ref=sr_1_8?ie=UTF8&qid=1502487183 &sr=8-8&keywords=Richard+W+Linford

426. JESUS CHRIST PAPERS. CHRISTMAS. EASTER. FATHER. SON. **CHRISTMAS AND EASTER OPUS: Honoring and testifying that GOD OUR HEAVENLY FATHER AND HIS BELOVED SON LIFE.**

427. JESUS CHRIST PAPERS. **COME KNEEL AT THE FEET OF GOD THE FATHER AND HIS SON JESUS CHRIST AND RECEIVE ETERNAL LIFE**

428. JESUS CHRIST PAPERS. **COME UNTO CHRIST: REPENT AND PRAY MIGHTILY FOR FORGIVENESS OF YOUR SINS! Meditations on Repentance, Prayer, and The Book of Mormon, Book of Enos: The Jesus Christ papers**
429. https://www.amazon.com/COME-UNTO-CHRIST-Forgiveness-MEDITATIONS-ebook/dp/B01N5HJFUW/ref=sr_1_12?ie=UTF8&qid=150583733 6&sr=8-12&keywords=Richard+W.+Linford

430. JESUS CHRIST PAPERS. DEATH. **DEATH SOLUTION: HOW TO AVOID YOUR DEATH?**

431. JESUS CHRIST PAPERS. ENEMIES. **How to get rid of your enemies?**

432. https://www.amazon.com/How-get-rid-your-enemies-ebook/dp/B01KVY0VK8/ref=sr_1_6?ie=UTF8&qid=1505837336&sr=8-6&keywords=Richard+W.+Linford

433. JESUS CHRIST PAPERS. GRANDPA TO GRANDSON. **A letter to my grandson, Jason: You are a son of our Heavenly Father and Mother. I love you. Your grandpa.**

434. JESUS CHRIST PAPERS. GRANDPA. GRANDSON. **GOD COULDN'T BE EVERYWHERE SO HE CREATED GRANDPAS: 692 WAYS TO BE A BETTER GRANDPA TO YOUR GRANDSON.**

435. JESUS CHRIST PAPERS. **HOLINESS! Worship the LORD in the Beauty of Holiness!**

436. https://www.amazon.com/HOLINESS-Worship-Beauty-Holiness-Christ-ebook/dp/B06XDHCBS6/ref=sr_1_29?ie=UTF8&qid=1502473575&sr=8-29&keywords=Richard+W+Linford

437. JESUS CHRIST PAPERS. **Honoring God the Son whose Second Coming is near: Holy Names, Titles and Concepts that describe Jehovah Jesus Christ The Holy Messiah**

438. https://www.amazon.com/Honoring-whose-Second-Coming-near/dp/1521473811/ref=sr_1_30?ie=UTF8&qid=1505838733&sr=8-30&keywords=Richard+W.+Linford

439. JESUS CHRIST PAPERS. **Honoring Moses and Thomas S. Monson, Prophets of God.**

440.https://www.amazon.com/Honoring-Moses-Thomas-Monson-Prophets/dp/1521399239/ref=sr_1_23?ie=UTF8&qid=1502473575&sr=8-23&keywords=Richard+W+Linford

441.<u>JESUS CHRIST PAPERS.</u> **Jesus Christ lives! The many witnesses: The Jesus Christ Papers Volume 1.**

442.<u>JESUS CHRIST PAPERS.</u> **Jesus Christ's True Church: 70 characteristics with scriptural references.**

443.<u>JESUS CHRIST PAPERS. LIFE. DEATH.</u> **he planted Utah strawberries and then he died: richard w Linford**
444.https://www.amazon.com/planted-utah-strawberries-then-died-ebook/dp/B00ZQ1OO64/ref=sr_1_28?ie=UTF8&qid=1502473575&sr=8-28&keywords=Richard+W+Linford

445.<u>JESUS CHRIST PAPERS. MARRIAGE.</u> **Choose Your Love! Love Your Choice! 22 Anti-divorce Principles for Christian Couples.**
446.**JESUS CHRIST PAPERS. MARION G. ROMNEY. HONORING PRESIDENT MARION G ROMNEY, Noble Apostle of Jesus the Christ the Holy Messiah,**https://www.amazon.com/s/ref=a9_sc_1?rh=i%3Aaps%2Ck%3Ahonoring+marion+g+romney&keywords=honoring+marion+g+romney&ie=UTF8&qid=1510957027

447.<u>JESUS CHRIST PAPERS.</u> **MEDITATIONS on "THE IMITATION OF CHRIST by Thomas A Kempis" BOOK ONE "Admonitions Profitable for the Spiritual Life": Translated by Rev. William Benham. Meditations by Richard W. Linford.**
https://www.amazon.com/MEDITATIONS-IMITATION-Admonitions-Profitable-Spiritual-ebook/dp/B01L2SANDW/ref=sr_1_4?ie=UTF8&qid=1502471298&sr=8-4&keywords=Richard+W.+Linford

448.<u>JESUS CHRIST PAPERS.</u> **Meditations on Jesus the Christ and the Book of Mormon, Book of Moroni - Come unto Christ and be perfected in Him. Read the Book of Mormon at <u>www.lds.org</u>. Ask God if these things are not true.**

449.https://www.amazon.com/Meditations-Jesus-Christ-Mormon-Moroni-ebook/dp/B01MDJT7R7/ref=sr_1_6?ie=UTF8&qid=1502484088&sr=8-6&keywords=richard+linford

450.JESUS CHRIST PAPERS. PEACE. **PUT DOWN YOUR THOUSAND STONES – Peace between Muslim, Jew and Christian – 304 thoughts - With all thy being, be at peace!**

451.JESUS CHRIST PAPERS. PERSECUTION. **HAUN'S MILL TREBLINKA TOO: The Persecution.**

452.JESUS CHRIST PAPERS. PRAYER. **PRAY ALWAYS TO OUR FATHER IN HEAVEN IN THE SACRED NAME OF HIS BELOVED SON JESUS CHRIST: The Purifying Power of Humble Prayer.**

453.JESUS CHRIST PAPERS. PRIESTHOOD KEYS. APOSTOLIC KEYS. **All Apostolic Keys of the Holy Priesthood and Kingdom of God were conferred upon the Prophet Joseph Smith.**

454.JESUS CHRIST PAPERS. REPENT. **Repent America or Be Destroyed Like the Jaredites! Repent and Serve The God of This Land who is Jesus Christ!**

455.JESUS CHRIST PAPERS. **THE HOLY GHOST. POWER AND GIFT. MEDITATIONS.**
456.https://www.amazon.com/Holy-Ghost-Power-Gift-Meditations-ebook/dp/B06W2KB7MZ/ref=sr_1_30?ie=UTF8&qid=1502473575&sr=8-30&keywords=Richard+W+Linford

457.JESUS CHRIST PAPERS. **THE MANY WITNESSES THAT "HE LIVES!"**
458.https://www.amazon.com/Jesus-Christ-Papers-Witnesses-Jehovah/dp/1575740214/ref=sr_1_35?ie=UTF8&qid=1505840223&sr=8-35&keywords=Richard+W.+Linford

459.JESUS CHRIST PAPERS. SABBATH BREAKING. **Sabbath Breaking and Sports as The Worlds' Religion: Fix it Richard!**
460.https://www.amazon.com/Sabbath-Breaking-Sports-Worlds-Religion-ebook/dp/B010MJFH06/ref=sr_1_31?ie=UTF8&qid=1502473575&sr=8-31&keywords=Richard+W+Linford

461.JESUS CHRIST PAPERS. **Would Jesus Christ Do That? Is the first question!**
462.https://www.amazon.com/Would-Jesus-Christ-first-question/dp/1575740168/ref=sr_1_25?ie=UTF8&qid=1505838470&sr=8-25&keywords=Richard+W.+Linford

463.MAKE MORE PEPPERONI "MONEY." **How to Make More Pepperoni?: How did Steven Jobs; Fed de Luca; Warren Buffett; Bill Gates; Larry Ellison; Carlos Slim; Fred, Charles, David Koch; do it.**

464.MATEO CERVANTES SERIES. NOVEL. **Mateo Cervantes - The Old Cowboy Prospector and The Buckskin Rocinante**

465.MELANIA TRUMP. **MELANIA TRUMP – HONORING FLOTUS.** https://www.amazon.com/MELANIA-TRUMP-Honoring-FLOTUS-intelligent/dp/1521995273/ref=sr_1_2?ie=UTF8&qid=1502471298&sr=8-2&keywords=Richard+W.+Linford

466.MARRIAGE. **199 Ways To Make Your Good Marriage Great or Your Bad marriage Better: Romance and improve your marriage today.**
467.https://www.amazon.com/Ways-Make-Marriage-Great-Better/dp/1575740184/ref=sr_1_14?ie=UTF8&qid=1502487183&sr=8-14&keywords=Richard+W+Linford

468.MONEY. **How to Make More Pepperoni? How did Steven Jobs; Fred de Luca; Warren Buffett; Bill Gates; Larry Ellison;**

Carlos Slim; Fred, Charles, David Koch; and the Waltons make more pepperoni and how can you?

469. https://www.amazon.com/How-Make-More-Pepperoni-pepperoni-ebook/dp/B011F4WZP2/ref=sr_1_9?ie=UTF8&qid=1502487183&sr=8-9&keywords=Richard+W+Linford

470. MUSTANGS. COWBOY POETRY. **Mustangs Running With The Judas Horse: How to Write Cowboy Poetry.**

471. OBAMACARE. **DID THE PATIENT DIE ON THE OPERATING TABLE? OBAMACARE 101 THOUGHTS: Is Obama's "Affordable Health Care" Plan Affordable? Is universal Health Care the answer?**

472. PERFORMANCE AND SUCCESS. **Push Your Limits! Honoring General John Francis Kelly! Semper Fidelis! [Always faithful! Always loyal!] The marines have landed at the US White House!**

473. https://www.amazon.com/Limits-Honoring-General-Francis-Fidelis/dp/1522066187/ref=sr_1_1?ie=UTF8&qid=1502471298&sr=8-1&keywords=Richard+W.+Linford

474. PERFORMANCE AND SUCCESS. **PUSH YOUR LIMITS! Honoring Ueli Steck with His two Golden Ice Axes In memoriam. A revolutionary way to live your life by challenging and speed climbing your seemingly impossible physical and spiritual mountains.**

475. https://www.amazon.com/limits-Honoring-Steck-Golden-memoriam-ebook/dp/B0727ZL9QS/ref=sr_1_10?ie=UTF8&qid=1502484088&sr=8-10&keywords=richard+linford

476. POLITICS. **DONALD TRUMP: 307 Promises and Positions**

477. https://www.amazon.com/DONALD-TRUMP-307-Promises-Positions-
ebook/dp/B01BWDHLVO/ref=sr_1_7?ie=UTF8&qid=150248718
3&sr=8-7&keywords=Richard+W+Linford

478. POLITICS. **50 Reasons to Honor President George W. Bush!: Even if you didn't vote for him!**
479. https://www.amazon.com/Reasons-Honor-President-George-Bush-
ebook/dp/B012PG4KSE/ref=sr_1_8?ie=UTF8&qid=1502484088
&sr=8-8&keywords=richard+linford

480. POLITICS. **Marty Mouse and The UK Brexit High Anxiety Hotel and Restaurant. A long story. An allegory.**
481. https://www.amazon.com/Marty-Mouse-Brexit-Anxiety-
Restaurant/dp/152109649X/ref=sr_1_27?ie=UTF8&qid=150247
3575&sr=8-27&keywords=Richard+W+Linford

482. POLITICS. **North Korea Solution – THE UNIFIED REPUBLIC OF KOREA! Tear down that DMZ wall Wise Leader Kim Jong-un! President Donald J. Trump.**
483. https://www.amazon.com/North-Korea-Solution-President-
peacefully/dp/1521131716/ref=sr_1_26?ie=UTF8&qid=1502473
575&sr=8-26&keywords=Richard+W+Linford

484. POLITICS. **THE ART OF THE STEAL – THE LITTLE RED POLITICAL BIBLE, ALMANAC, AND CAMPAIGN HANDBOOK. 237 LESSONS FROM THE 2015-2016 TRUMP AND OTHER AMERICAN POLITICAL CAMPAIGNS.**
485. https://www.amazon.com/ART-STEAL-POLITICAL-2015-2016-CAMPAIGNS-
ebook/dp/B01E7K829E/ref=sr_1_15?ie=UTF8&qid=1502487183
&sr=8-15&keywords=Richard+W+Linford

486. <u>RAINMAKING.</u> BUSINESS DEVELOPMENT. **RAINMAKER, WHO STOPPED THE RAIN DANCE AND TURNED OFF MY RAIN? Rainmaking for lawyers and non-lawyers.**
487. https://www.amazon.com/RAINMAKER-STOPPED-RAIN-DANCE-TURNED-ebook/dp/B00Q7QH9NC/ref=sr_1_11?ie=UTF8&qid=1502487183&sr=8-11&keywords=Richard+W+Linford

488. <u>SILENCE.</u> **In Search of Silence.**
489. https://www.amazon.com/Search-Silence-521-quiet-thoughts-ebook/dp/B01M7UCRX8/ref=sr_1_10?ie=UTF8&qid=1505837336&sr=8-10&keywords=Richard+W.+Linford

490. <u>SPEED LEARNING. SPEED READING.</u> **Speed Learning Checklists: How to speed learn your way to greater expertise and fortune.**
491. https://www.amazon.com/Speed-Learning-Checklists-greater-expertise-ebook/dp/B0106L853G/ref=sr_1_11?ie=UTF8&qid=1505837336&sr=8-11&keywords=Richard+W.+Linford

492. <u>SUPER POWERS.</u> **Andy Pepper and Prince Kahlid's Solid Gold Western Flyer X-53: A novelette.**

493. <u>SURVIVAL CHECKLIST HANDBOOK.</u>
494. https://www.amazon.com/SURVIVAL-CHECKLIST-HANDBOOK-Principles-Checklists-ebook/dp/B00PXLSD6E/ref=sr_1_15?ie=UTF8&qid=1505837336&sr=8-15&keywords=Richard+W.+Linford

495. <u>TESTOSTERONE.</u> ABS. ED. LOW **TESTOSTERONE, ED, AND 6-8 PACK ABS: 558 thoughts to help you maintain and increase your T, overcome ED, and build 608 Pack Abs.**
496. https://www.amazon.com/LOW-TESTOSTERONE-6-8-PACK-ABS-

ebook/dp/B01BCX3Q90/ref=sr_1_16?ie=UTF8&qid=150583733
6&sr=8-16&keywords=Richard+W.+Linford

**497. THINK. Think and Grow Smart! Think and Grow Rich! The
Story of Ineptitude and the foolish cutting of the Golconda
Great Mogul Diamond – The Largest Diamond Found in India
Coupled with 50 Tried and True Ancient and Modern
Knowledge and Wealth Wisdom Principles**
498. https://www.amazon.com/Think-Grow-Smart-Rich-
Principles/dp/1521710155/ref=sr_1_21?ie=UTF8&qid=1502473
575&sr=8-21&keywords=Richard+W+Linford

**499. TIME. Waiting with Brutus Caesar Anthony the 7th and
William and Mary Waiting for SAM THE MECHANIC MAN, A
long story. An allegory for our auto-driven times. I write. You
read. You decide.**
500. https://www.amazon.com/Waiting-Brutus-Anthony-
William-
MECHANIC/dp/1521158010/ref=sr_1_25?ie=UTF8&qid=150247
3575&sr=8-25&keywords=Richard+W+Linford

**501. UNICORN. The White Unicorn Code: Mystery of the Lady
with the Unicorn and other Unicorn tapestries**

**503. WEIGHT REDUCTION. HIGH FRUCTOSE CORN SYRUP AND
SUGAR BELLY: 550 thoughts to help you lose your ugly fat and
rip your set of six or eight pack abs no matter your age!**

**504. WORLD PRISON REFORM SOLUTIONS? 2016 – 2017
INDUSTRIAL RESEARCH REPORT In Search of Prison Reform --
Are our prisons an ethical stain on American society?**
505. https://www.amazon.com/WORLD-PRISON-REFORM-
SOLUTIONS-2016-
ebook/dp/B01N3LDTJ5/ref=sr_1_7?ie=UTF8&qid=1505837336&
sr=8-7&keywords=Richard+W.+Linford

506. <u>WORLD ANTI-TERRORISM SOLUTIONS</u> IN SEARCH OF POSITIVE WAYS TO ELIMINATE TERRORISM 2016 – 2017 COUNTER TERRORISM RESEARCH REPORT 1st Edition

507. <u>WORLD WATER SOLUTIONS?</u> 2016 – 2017 INDUSTRIAL RESEARCH REPORT: AIR TO WATER MACHINES. This Industrial Report surveys information available about Air to Water Machines and Air to Water Technology and begins after paragraph 54.

508. <u>ER SOLUTIONS?</u> 2016 – 2017 INDUSTRIAL RESEARCH REPORT: CHEAP? WATER PURIFICATION, SALT WATER DESALINATION, ATMOSPHERIC WATER GENERATION
509. https://www.amazon.com/WORLD-WATER-SOLUTIONS-2016-PURIFICATION-ebook/dp/B01M12XHTA/ref=sr_1_32?ie=UTF8&qid=1502473575&sr=8-32&keywords=Richard+W+Linford

510. **The author**

511. **Richard works at being a decent husband, dad, brother, grandpa, Church and Community service person, family history and genealogy person, attorney at law, businessman, auditor, writer, publisher, blogger, speaker, trainer, oil and acrylic artist, gardener, and wannabe golfer.**

512. **He is a member of The Church of Jesus Christ of Latter-day Saints (The Mormons).**

513. **He served a 3 year proselyting mission to the Netherlands and Belgium, several years as a lay bishop, as a member of an LDS Stake Presidency for 13 years, as LDS Region Welfare Executive Secretary and Specialist, as a member of the Melchizedek Priesthood General Committee for the LDS**

Church, as guide on LDS Temple Square, and as a member of the Salt Lake Inner City Mission leadership.

514. He currently serves as a Salt Lake LDS Temple worker, and as the Volunteers Active in Disaster (VOAD) Representative and Welfare Specialist for the LDS Church for the state of Utah.

515. He is former chairman of the board of the Salt Lake, South Davis, Tooele, and Summit multi-county Red Cross.

516. He served on Junior Achievement, Lowell Bennion Community Service, and Utah American Heart Association boards.

517. He served as a member of the Board of Fellows of Southern Utah State University.

518. He served 14 years as a state and national board member, and state chairman, of The National Conference of Christians, Jews, and Muslims.

519. He served as an LDS Church Education seminary and institute instructor, director, and curriculum writer, as director of Program Development and Marketing Services in the LDS Welfare Services Department, as an LDS Church Auditor, as Director of Operations and Director of 16,000 Public Affairs Directors in the LDS Church Public Affairs Department, as Assistant to the President and Vice President of Bonneville International Broadcasting Corporation, as CEO of Bonneville Entertainment Company, Media Paymaster plus, and InteliQuest Learning Systems, as a President and CEO and Chairman of the Board of InteliQuest Media Corporation, and

as an owner of KIQ AM 1010 50,000 watt news talk radio station.

520. He co-produced audio and print programs The World's 100 Greatest Books, The World's 100 Greatest People, and The World's 50 Greatest Composers, their lives and their music.

521. He operates several blogs and has written more than 60 books and painted more than 600 oil and acrylic paintings.

522. **BLOG.** You can read his conservative blog at POTUSWARS™ www.richlinfordreport.com.

523. **ART.** You can view his art – more than 600 oil and acrylic paintings catalogued in galleries -- at FineArtAmerica. www.richard-w-linford.pixels.com

524. **BOOKS.** His books are found at www.amazon.com. Type his name Richard W. Linford.

www.ingramcontent.com/pod-product-compliance
Lightning Source LLC
Chambersburg PA
CBHW070812240726
48654CB00007B/314